Access Your Online Resources

The *Staying Well Activity Book* is accompanied by a number of printable online materials, designed to ensure this resource best suits your needs.

The **Goodbye Card**, **Glitter Jar**, **Coping Spinner**, and **Awards Ceremony** pages are available online to be downloaded and printed for easy use.

Go to https://resourcecentre.routledge.com/speechmark and click on the cover of this book.

Answer the questions prompt using your copy of the book to gain access to the online content.

"Claire Holmes has crafted a masterpiece. It should be a gift from every school to every single student aged 7–12 who will see a friend move away at the end of the year. Too often the adults' attention goes to the students and families packing their bags and boxes. This book fills a long overdue gap in the hearts and minds of the stayers. We have long suspected that the unresolved losses associated with being 'a stayer' can impact the ability of these students to make and maintain long-term emotional bonds with others. Claire's book addresses this gap, with a storehouse of accessible tricks and tools. Do not be mistaken by the playfulness of her approach: it is based on sound psychological science mixing mindfulness, cognitive therapy, and polyvagal theory. This book will help kids stay well and fully reap the benefits of a life where change happens. We owe Claire Holmes a debt of gratitude for writing it."
Dr. Douglas W. Ota, *author of* Safe Passage: How mobility affects people & what international schools should do about it. *Founder, Safe Passage Across Networks (SPAN), psychologist, presenter, consultant, researcher*.

"*Staying Well* is a true gem for kids facing difficult times. The activity book's creative approach makes it not just a book but a canvas for young minds to explore their emotions and questions and build their resilience. It's a practical guide that fosters self-reflection and personal growth whilst providing a platform for nurture and support at a difficult time. The *Facilitator's Guide* is a reassuring companion for adults, equipping them with all the tools and insights to be the supportive rock a child needs during times of loss and change. These books are engaging and incredibly valuable, providing children and their supporting adults with the resources they need to navigate life's changes and challenges. A must-have for anyone supporting a child whose friend is moving away."
Dr. Pooky Knightsmith, *world-renowned expert on mental health, author, keynote speaker and advisor*.

Staying Well Activity Book

Coping when a friend moves away is hard. This book is designed to help 'the stayers' (those left behind) manage this big change. Perfect for children aged 7–12, it's jam-packed full of activities that invite the reader to use their creativity by annotating and illustrating the pages. This makes the book unique to each child, helping them feel a greater sense of agency and control at a time of change.

The text acknowledges change is stressful and the child is encouraged to think about their own responses to change and build their coping repertoire. The concept of TRUST is introduced, an acronym for five key things to 'stay well'. The reader explores what each letter stands for and considers how paying attention to these can help make their process smoother. The book concludes with activities that bring together the child's journey through the pages, helping to solidify their learning and engagement with the text.

Best introduced around eight weeks before the friend leaves, this is a must-have resource to help children 'stay well'. Grounded in wellbeing and transition research, this activity book contains much wisdom for adults too.

Claire Holmes is a school counsellor; her approach is trauma-informed and strength-based, empowering others to access their inner wisdom and knowing. As a mindfulness teacher, she weaves meditation into her work, alongside expressive therapies, and solution-focused interventions. She delights in spending time in the great outdoors and is a Nature and Forest Therapy Guide in training. She's passionate about positive transitions, having lived and worked in Singapore for over two decades, and understands first-hand what it means to be 'a stayer'. She is the author of the *Moving On* series and is delighted to add the *Staying Well* books to her collection.

This book is part of a set –

Book 1: *Staying Well Activity Book* is jam-packed full of strategies and creative activities to help 'the stayer' reflect on how they feel, appreciate their friendship, and build a coping repertoire.

Book 2: *Staying Well Facilitator's Guide* offers guidance notes and prompts to help bring out the best experience for the child and is designed to help the lead-adult feel confident in their delivery and in responding to any questions. It contains key points to consider, examples of 'what you could say', and explains the theory behind the activities.

Staying Well Activity Book

Practical Activities to Support Children Aged 7–12 whose Best Friend is Leaving

Claire Holmes

Routledge
Taylor & Francis Group

LONDON AND NEW YORK

Cover credit: Hana Holmes (design) and Lisa Dynan (illustrator)

First published 2025
by Routledge
4 Park Square, Milton Park, Abingdon, Oxon OX14 4RN

and by Routledge
605 Third Avenue, New York, NY 10158

Routledge is an imprint of the Taylor & Francis Group, an informa business

British Library Cataloguing-in-Publication Data
A catalogue record for this book is available from the British Library

ISBN: 978-1-032-70438-8 (pbk)
ISBN: 978-1-032-70440-1 (ebk)

This book is part of the *Staying Well* set, ISBN: 9781032663548

DOI: 10.4324/9781032704401

Typeset in Tekton Pro
by KnowledgeWorks Global Ltd.

Access the Support Material: https://resourcecentre.routledge.com/speechmark

Dedication:

This book is dedicated to my two children, Hana and Ben. They have been 'stayers' far too often over the years. May you both grow resilience and perspective from your experiences, laugh, love, and be happy.

Acknowledgments:

Heartfelt thanks to my husband Chris for always encouraging me in my hairbrained endeavours. Appreciation goes out to my close friends who have moved away, taught me how to be 'the stayer,' and helped me understand the value of true friendship, you know who you are. Thanks to my school counselling colleagues, past and present, much of your inspiration is in these pages, you are all awesome. Lastly to my ever-wise counselling supervisor, Helen Wilson, you are my guru.

Welcome!

You've been given this activity book because your best friend is leaving. It's hard being 'the stayer' who is left behind. It's a book that helps you share how you feel and learn ways to cope with change. Each page has a different activity. You'll get creative by drawing, colouring, writing, and making things. The last page is a 'brain dump' page for you to plan anything you need to.

This book belongs to _____

My friend's name who is leaving is _____

They are moving to _____

Goodbyes may not be forever; they may not be the end; they simply mean farewell until you meet again.

Change happens.

Change is a normal part of life; nothing stays the same forever. Perhaps you have moved from one school to another, moved house, or from one sports team to another. Your friend leaving is another big change, and it will take time to adjust.

Fill in the gaps... a change I remember is:

from _____ to _____

Draw something above to go with this change.

Write something below that helped you cope:

What stays the same and what changes?

When your friend leaves some things will stay the same and some will change – write or draw these things below:

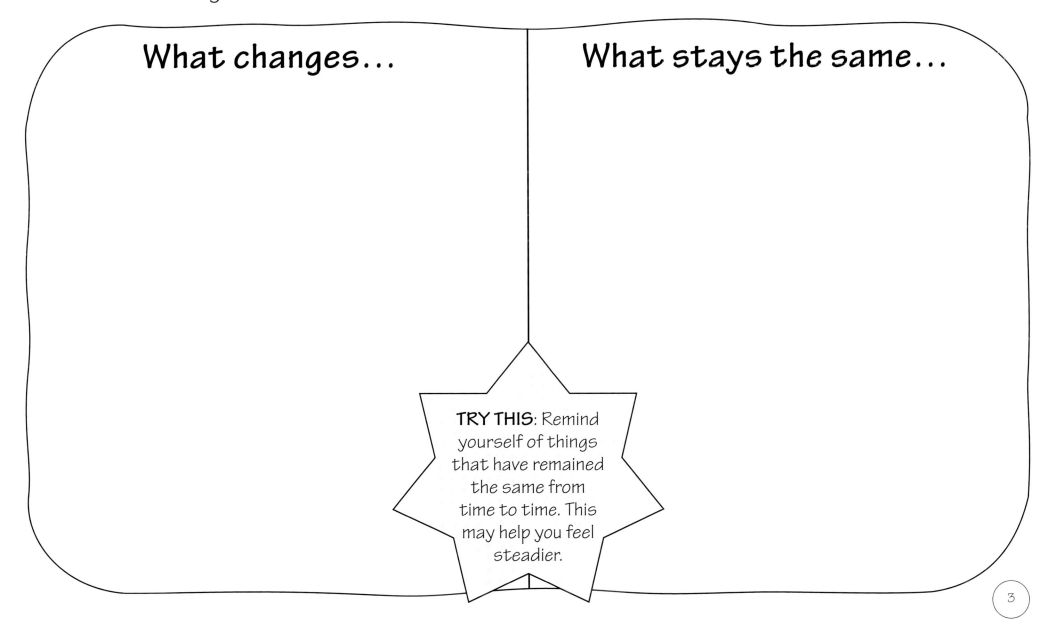

What changes…

What stays the same…

TRY THIS: Remind yourself of things that have remained the same from time to time. This may help you feel steadier.

Friendship facts.

Draw something to represent your friend in the left-hand circle and yourself in the right. You may choose to draw colours, shapes, lines, squiggles or draw an object, portrait, or hobby. On the three lines below the left-hand circle write three character traits you like about your friend, and on the right-hand lines write three things you like about yourself when you are with your friend.

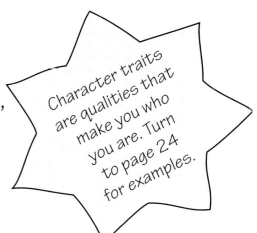

Character traits are qualities that make you who you are. Turn to page 24 for examples.

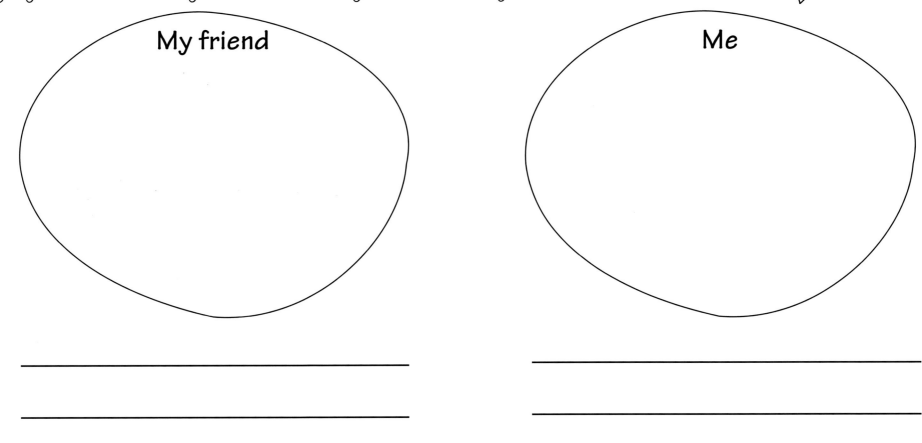

My friend

Me

Magic memories: highlight reel.

There are five spaces on the highlight reel below to write or draw happy memories you have with your friend.

Technique means a special way of doing something you can practise.

TRY THIS: Magic Memories Technique. You may like to tune in more deeply to these happy times. Close your eyes, take a breath, and imagine yourself and your friend in one of your memories above. Tune into your five senses as you do this by noticing what you could see, hear, touch, smell, and taste at the time of your chosen memory. Take a deep breath and open your eyes. Repeat for your other highlight reel memories if you wish.

Staying Well takes TRUST.

Each letter of the word **T-R-U-S-T** stands for something that will help 'stay well' when your friend is leaving. Paying attention to each letter will help you grow your **TRUST** and cope in the best way for you.

Take care of you

Remain in contact

Unload feelings

Say goodbye

Take opportunities

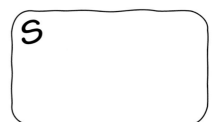

Draw something in each of the five blocks on the left to represent what each letter stands for.

6

T

T is for? _____

Wellbeing scales.

An important part of taking care of you is doing activities you enjoy. You might not want to do them as much when your friend is leaving but these things boost your wellbeing and help you cope better with change.

Wellbeing is a state of feeling comfortable, happy, and healthy.

Write down or draw things you enjoy in this box:

TRY THIS:
Choose to do things in your box to lift your mood.

Your Wellbeing is not always the same, it moves up and down. Some days you'll feel better than others.

Take Care of You

How do I cope well?

TRY THIS: Rank each of the strategies below, 1–10. Number 10 being the most helpful. Write your number in the circle inside each box.

Colour in the squares below which contain things that might steady yourself when you feel stressed about your friend's move. Different people find different things helpful.

Take five deep breaths.	Listen to music, play an instrument, or watch a movie.	Get a drink of water and/or splash cold water on your face.	Play with a favourite pet, friend, or toy.	Imagine a beautiful and peaceful place.
Talk with a trusted adult or friend.	Move your body however you like e.g. do some jumping jacks, play outside, or skip.	Say something calming to yourself like: "It's okay, I've got this."	Write down or draw how you are feeling.	Do some art or make something.

Add one more of your own here: _____

Saying encouraging things to myself.

Speaking to yourself with kind words helps lift your mood and cope when the going gets tough. Write some encouraging messages to say to yourself when you feel worried or upset about your friend leaving in speech bubbles 1–4. Ask a supportive adult to write you a message to say to yourself in speech bubble 5 and ask your friend who is leaving to write an encouraging message in speech bubble 6.

TRY THIS: Come back to this page when you feel upset. Read the messages to yourself. Take a big, deep breath after each one.

Rainbow breathing.

Begin by colouring in the rainbow on this page, make each layer of the rainbow a different colour.

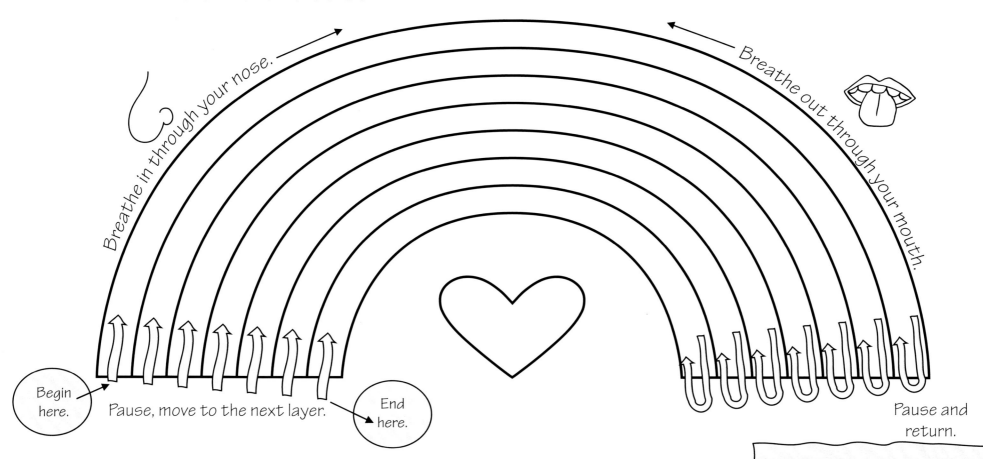

Breathe in through your nose.

Breathe out through your mouth.

Begin here.

Pause, move to the next layer.

End here.

Pause and return.

TRY THIS: Place your finger on 'begin here.' Follow the arrow and trace across the first layer of the rainbow with your finger, breathe in through your nose as you do this. When you get to the other side, pause, and follow the arrow back, tracing your finger across the same layer of the rainbow, breathing out through your mouth. Repeat for each layer of the rainbow. Use this technique as many times as you need to steady yourself.

TRY THIS: Practice Rainbow breathing when you feel okay. When you get used to it, try it when you want to take care of big feelings.

Taking my pencil for a walk.

Find a pencil you'd like to draw with. Start your drawing anywhere on this page by touching your pencil to the paper. Begin to doodle on the page by moving your pencil around but do not lift it off the page until you feel your drawing is done. You might like to play your favourite music as you do this. See where your hand guides you. Relax, take slow, deep breaths, and enjoy your creativity.

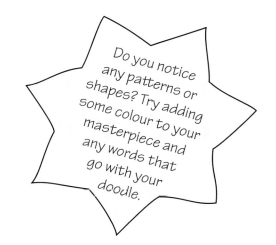

Do you notice any patterns or shapes? Try adding some colour to your masterpiece and any words that go with your doodle.

 TRY THIS: Do this again on another piece of paper if you enjoyed it.

Take Care of You

My **circle** of support.

These circles will help you think of supportive people who can help you get through this time of change. Draw a picture of yourself in the centre. In the next layer, write or draw family members and then friends in the next. In the outer circle, people in the community, these could be teachers/ staff members at school, coaches/tutors/ therapists, or others.

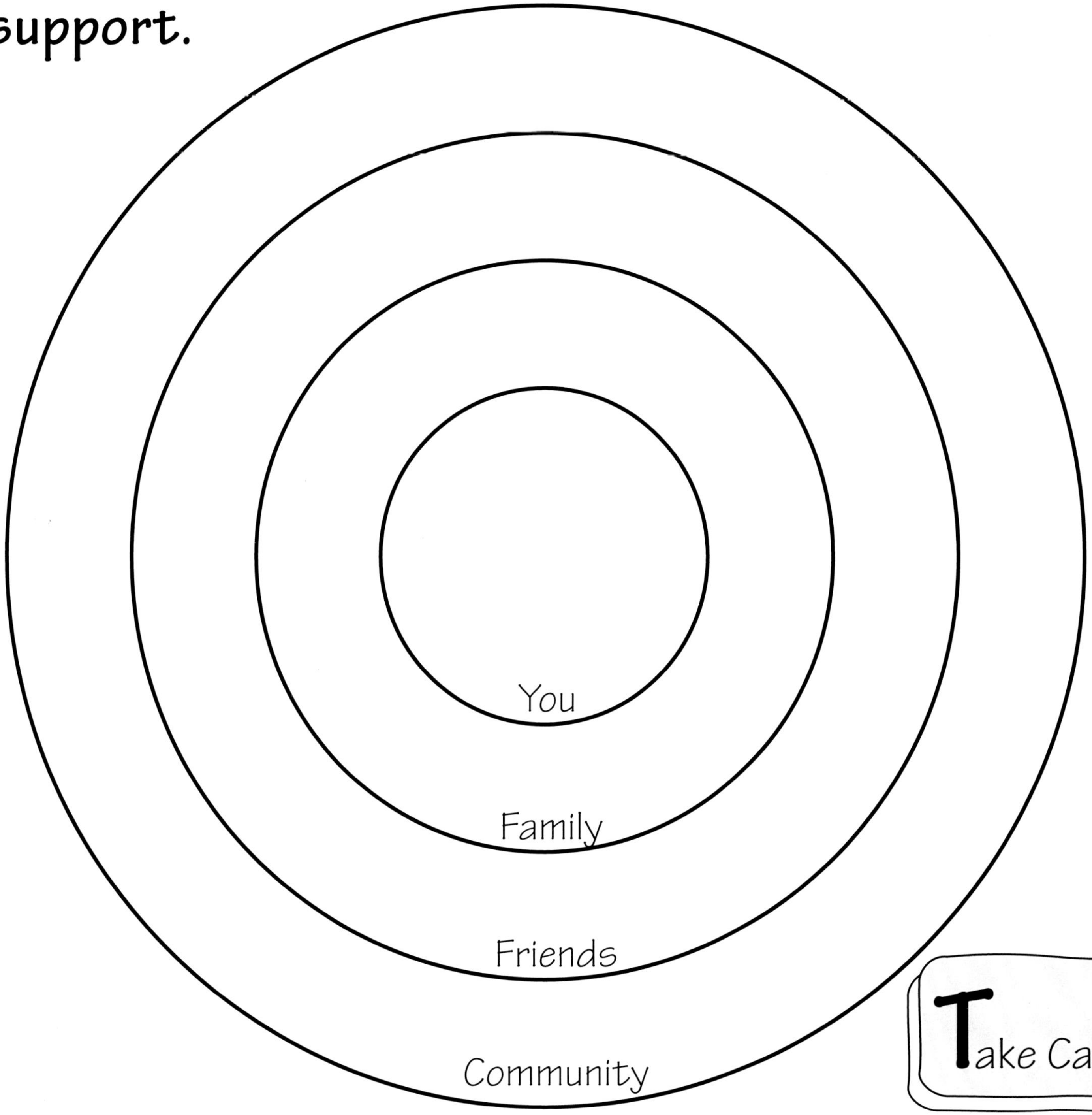

You

Family

Friends

Community

Take Care of You

The magic of vitamin N (N = NATURE).

Spending time in nature lifts your mood. A walk is a good way to be active in nature. Being still in nature, listening to sounds, noticing smells, textures, and what you *see* increases wellbeing. Caring for plants can be a great wellbeing boost too.

1) TRY THIS: Your imagination is powerful. Close your eyes and think carefully about a special place in nature - real or imagined - and your body, heart, and mind will be positively impacted. Try it now, as you imagine your place notice what you can see, hear, touch, taste, and smell as if you were there. Practice this when you feel okay to begin with to get used to it.

2) NOW, TRY THIS:

Use colours, shapes, lines, and/or squiggles to represent your place in nature from the activity on the left. Add words too if you wish:

R is for? _____

Creative connections.

Planning how you will stay in touch with your friend increases the chances of remaining connected. Get creative with this! You might send care packages, write letters, visit them, and/or stay connected through technology.

Write or draw some ideas below of how you will stay in touch with your friend. Add any important information like their home address, email, their birthday, or social media information:

U 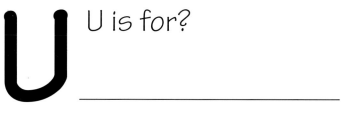 U is for?

_____

What my body tells me.

Noticing how your body tells you big feelings have arrived helps to feel more in control.

Below are some feelings, colour in the box next to the feeling with a colour. Add other feelings on the empty lines. Next, using your chosen colours for each feeling, draw on the body outline on the right, shapes, lines, and/or squiggles to show where and how each feeling shows up in your body. Add words if you wish.

Sad

Happy

Angry

Peaceful

Worried

Confident

_____

_____

TRY THIS: Notice what your body is telling you and name the feeling. This helps be in control. Try tuning into your body, what feeling is here right now?

Draw feelings out.

Unload feelings

Choose one of the feelings from the last page.

Write the feeling here: _____.

Answer the questions below and draw your feeling in the box.

Where do you feel it in your body? _____

Does your feeling have a colour? _____

Does it have a shape? _____

How big or small is it? _____

Is it moving or still? _____

Does it have a temperature? _____

Does it have a texture, smell, and/or taste?

_____

A sound? _____

Anything else to say about your feeling? _____

_____

Draw your feeling here:

Feelings focus.

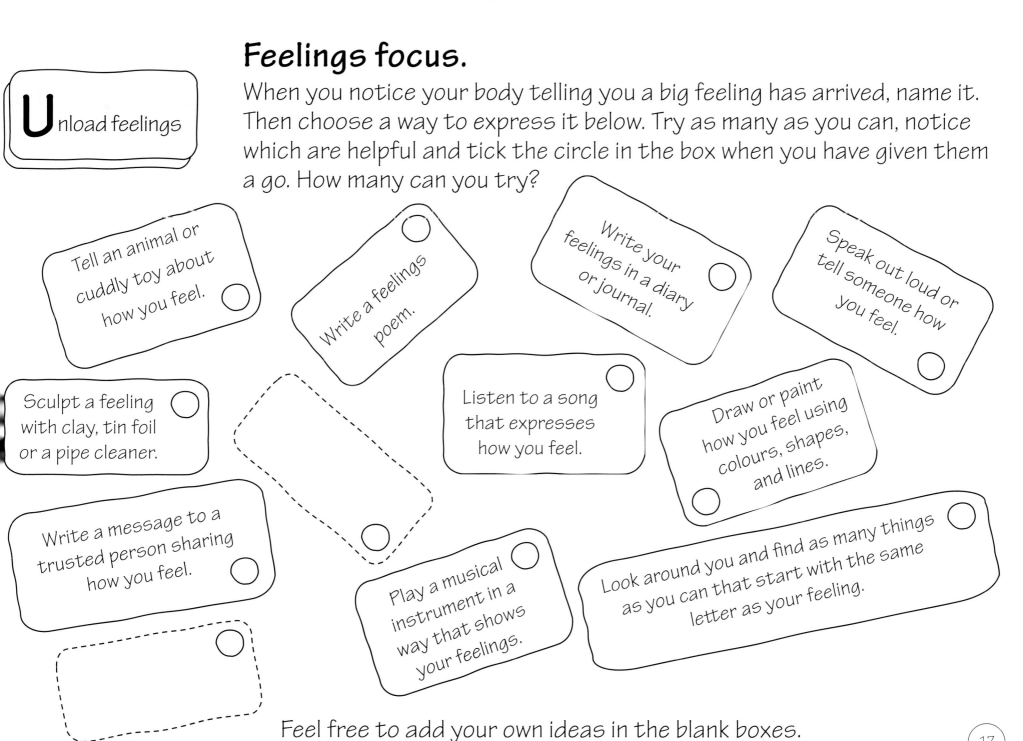

Unload feelings

When you notice your body telling you a big feeling has arrived, name it. Then choose a way to express it below. Try as many as you can, notice which are helpful and tick the circle in the box when you have given them a go. How many can you try?

Tell an animal or cuddly toy about how you feel.

Write a feelings poem.

Write your feelings in a diary or journal.

Speak out loud or tell someone how you feel.

Sculpt a feeling with clay, tin foil or a pipe cleaner.

Listen to a song that expresses how you feel.

Draw or paint how you feel using colours, shapes, and lines.

Write a message to a trusted person sharing how you feel.

Play a musical instrument in a way that shows your feelings.

Look around you and find as many things as you can that start with the same letter as your feeling.

Feel free to add your own ideas in the blank boxes.

17

Gratitude banner.

Feeling grateful helps to notice the good, and what we notice, we get more of. Write or draw five things you are grateful for in each of the flags of the banner below.

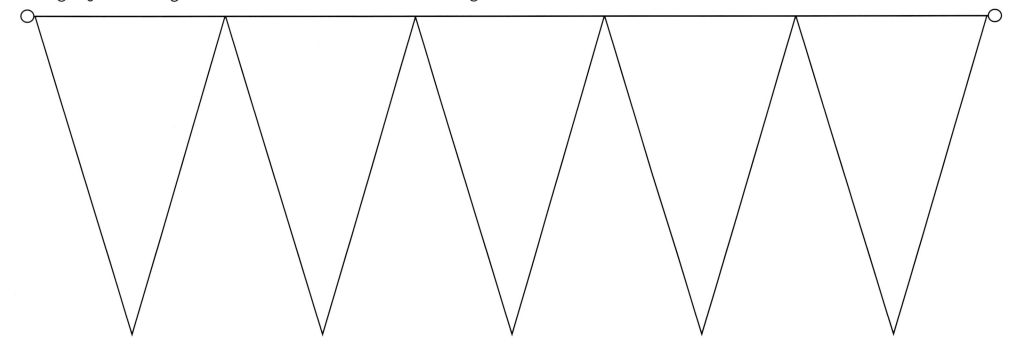

TRY THIS:

1) Read or say what is on your first flag out loud; "I am grateful for… (say what's on your flag)"
2) Close your eyes and imagine whatever is on that flag.
3) Take a big breath in through your nose and breathe out through your mouth.

REPEAT FOR THE REST OF THE FLAGS.

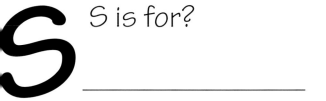

S _____

S is for?

There is still time to make your farewell 'highlight reel moments'!

Purposeful planning.

It's best to plan how to say goodbye in advance of your friend leaving so you bid farewell in the right way for you both. Planning a special event, writing cards/giving gifts are some ideas, write some below that fit for you.

Where?

What?

When?

Where?

What?

When?

Where?

What?

When?

Where?

What?

When?

Show your parent/s or guardians your plan/s to see what's possible. Talk about what needs to be done. Sometimes plans need a bit of adjustment!

Goodbye Card for my friend.

Use this page to plan a goodbye card for your friend. This is a chance to celebrate your friendship and show your friend how important they are to you. Everyone's card will be unique and special, no two cards will be the same. Focus on happy memories, positive things about your friend and your friendship, and strengths you notice in them.

⬇ Create your design for the front in this half. ⬇   ⬇ Write your message in this half. ⬇

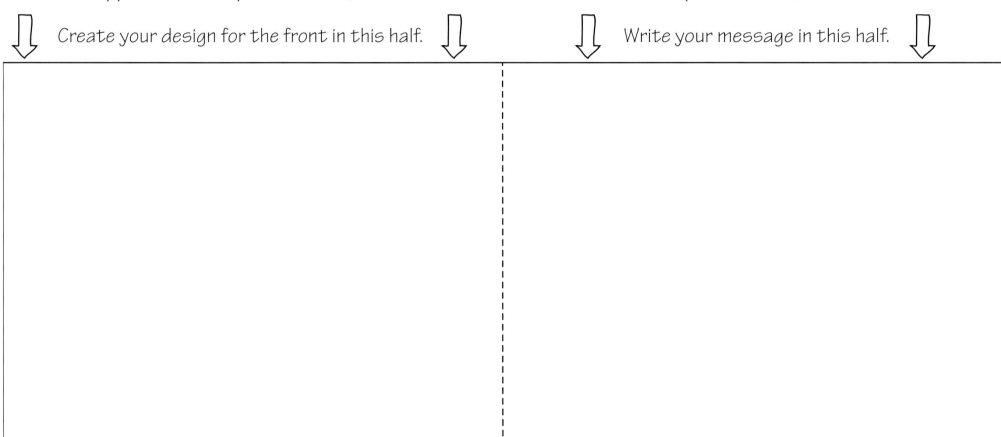

After your planning, create the real thing. You can use your own card or download this template from *The Staying Well Activity Book Support Material.* Once it's ready, find a special moment to give it to your friend.

A message from my friend.

Ask your friend who is leaving if they would be willing to write you a note and/or draw you a picture on this page.

T

T is for?

_____

Cool connections.

The last letter of **TRUST** requires you to be brave by taking opportunities to get to know people better, make new friends and/or try new things.

Top tips for making connections

#1 Smile and be friendly

#2 Ask people about themselves and listen

#3 Find others with shared interests

#4 Be brave, make the first move

#5 Be YOU

Can you add a couple of your own?

#6

#7

Notice each time you connect by trying one of the top tips above. Keep doing what works!

List activities/events/situations below you could try/join to connect with others, they might be new things or things you already do:

☐

☐

☐

☐

☐

☐

Tick each activity off when you have tried them.

REMEMBER: It's normal to have some setbacks – be patient, making connections takes time.

What's in and out of my control?

1) Get a pencil ready.

2) Place your hand, palm down, over the words 'Things I can control on this page.'

3) Carefully draw around your hand.

4) Write or draw things you CAN control inside the hand you have drawn; examples might be 'my breathing' or 'how I speak to people'.

5) Write or draw things you CAN'T control outside the hand; examples might be 'how friends behave' or 'the weather'.

6) Add things you CAN and CAN'T control about your friend leaving.

Things I can't control

Things I can control

Appreciating strengths.

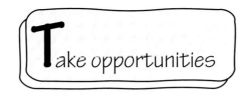

Take opportunities

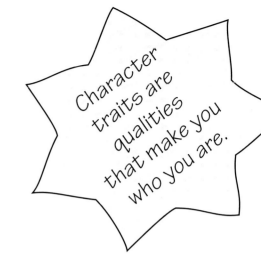

Character traits are qualities that make you who you are.

Strengths are positive character traits that you and others notice. Using your strengths helps you be the best version of yourself.

Here are some examples of strengths:

Kind, caring, funny, patient, trusting, friendly, grateful, loyal, helpful, joyful, honest, determined, brave, creative, respectful, and peaceful.

Write other strengths you can think of here:

Star strengths.

This page helps you think about your strengths you and others notice.

1) Write your own strengths inside the star. Aim for eight or more!

2) In the box below, write three strengths you wrote in your star that are most important to help you cope with your friend leaving.

3) In the box below, write one strength that you did not add to your star that would help you to 'stay well'.

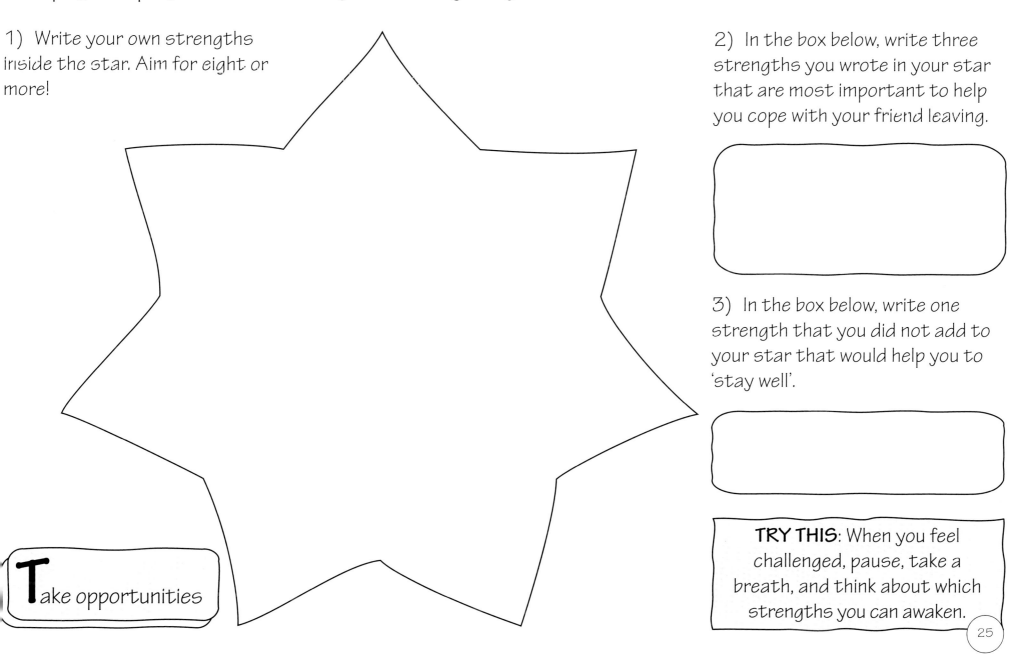

Take opportunities

TRY THIS: When you feel challenged, pause, take a breath, and think about which strengths you can awaken.

Staying Well podium.

The activities in this book have helped to awaken your **T-R-U-S-T**. Write down three things you'd like to remember from this *Staying Well Activity Book* in the boxes below. Rank them 1–3 with number 1 being the most helpful.

1

2

3

Make a Glitter Jar.

When you have made your jar, you can use it to settle your mind and help you relax. The glitter in your jar is like thoughts in your mind. When you feel stressed, your mind gets all churned up. When you are calm your mind is more settled.

Gather your 'ingredients':

- 1 airtight jar with lid
- Warm water
- Clear glue
- Lollypop stick
- Glitter, various colours and sizes.

Making your jar:

1) Prepare some warm water.
2) Pour enough glitter into the jar to generously cover the bottom.
3) Add a big dollop of clear glue.
4) Add enough warm water to cover the glitter and glue and stir with the lollypop stick.
5) Put the lid on the jar and shake well.
6) Take the lid off and add water to the top, replace the lid and shake again.

Optional – Add the label at the top right of this page to the lid of your jar

Cut out the label below and stick it on your jar lid.

**GLITTER JAR
(DO NOT DRINK ME)**

The glitter in this jar is like thoughts in your mind. When you feel stressed, your mind gets churned up. When you are calm your mind is more settled.

TO STEADY YOURSELF:
1) Shake your jar.
2) Watch the glitter settle whilst you breathe slowly.

How to use your jar:

- Find a comfortable space
- Take a deep breath
- Shake your jar
- Watch the glitter settle as you breathe slowly.
- Take another deep breath.

Make a Coping Spinner.

The back of this page is blank so that you can cut out the circles. You may prefer to download them instead.

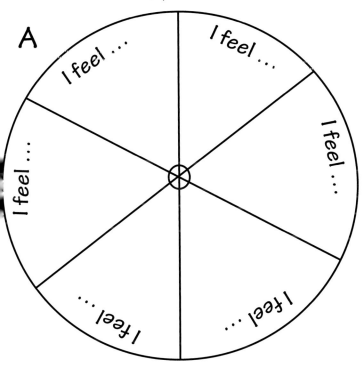

A

I feel …
I feel …
I feel …
I feel …
I feel …
I feel …

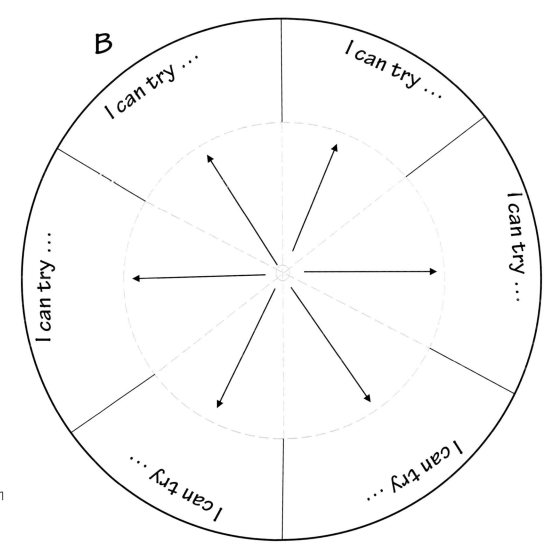

B

I can try …
I can try …
I can try …
I can try …
I can try …
I can try …

1) Add six feelings that are tricky to deal with to each section of the circle A (use page 15 to help you.) Then cut out the circle.

2) Flick through this activity book and choose six coping skills you have learnt, write/draw them, one in each of the outer section of circle B. Then cut out the circle.

3) Place the small circle on top of the big circle in the centre. Push a paper fastener, pencil, or paperclip through the middle so that the two circles can turn.

TRY THIS: When big feelings arrive, choose a feeling from the small circle and say, 'I feel… (whatever the feeling is).' Next spin the spinner to line up the feeling with one of your coping strategies in the outer ring, say 'I can try… (whatever the strategy is).' You can do this with your eyes closed or even use dice to determine how many moves you make. Then do the chosen strategy. Repeat if you would like another go.

Awards Ceremony.

Read the stickers below. Choose a page that goes with each of them. Colour in the sticker, cut it out and glue it onto your chosen page.

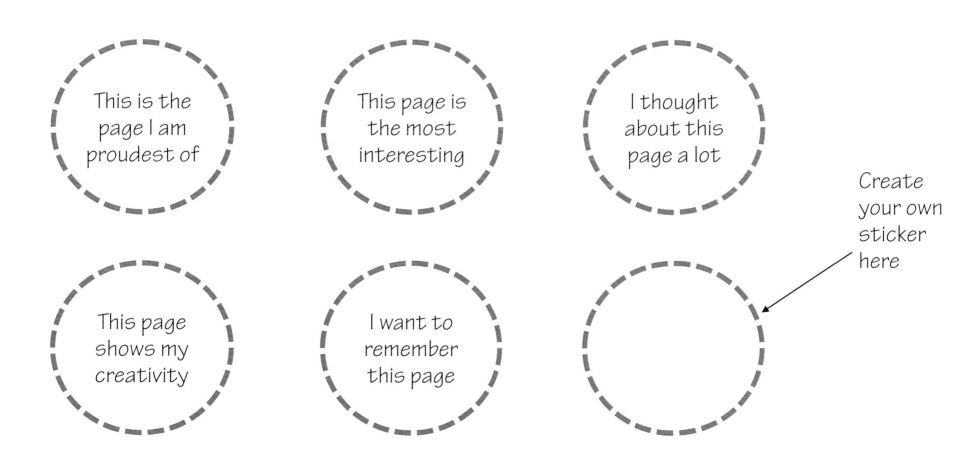

This is the page I am proudest of

This page is the most interesting

I thought about this page a lot

Create your own sticker here

This page shows my creativity

I want to remember this page

The back of this page is blank so that you can cut out the circles. You may prefer to download them instead from *The Staying Well Activity Book Support Material* online.

'Brain-dump' page. Add any thoughts, scribbles, or notes: